EXCAVATION OF THE SOUL

REDISCOVERING THE GOD WHO NEVER LEFT

G. WRAY

Excavation of the Soul

Published by Wray of Light Publishing

ISBN: 978-1-968631-02-4

First Edition, 2025

For inquiries, permissions, or speaking invitations:

✉ gwray@tuta.com

Table of Contents

Dedication

To my wife—
my sounding board, my encourager,
and my most patient friend.

Thank you for your unwavering feedback,
for your grace as I wrestled with words,
and for the time you gave so I could chase this calling.

Your prayers never ceased,
and your faith allowed the
Holy Spirit to guide me when I needed it most.

This book bears your quiet wisdom on every page—
thank you for shaping it with me.

With all my gratitude and love

Preface

There are quiet moments—
sometimes painful, sometimes holy—
when something shifts.

Not all at once.
Not with lightning.

But deep beneath the surface, something
you once trusted begins to tremble.

The frame still stands.
But the foundation?
It doesn't feel like bedrock anymore.

You still believe in God.
You still love Jesus.

But the structure that once held
your faith—whether theology, habit,
or self-understanding—
has begun to lean.

Maybe it's been leaning for a long time.
This book is for people like us.

Not for those who've walked away entirely—
but for those who still show up.
Still pray.
Still care.
And still feel the ache of something missing.

For those who've tried to hold it all together…
and finally realized they can't.

This is not a deconstruction manual.
It's not a fix-yourself formula.
And it's not a call to return to the
old ways that never quite fit.

This is an excavation.
A sacred digging.

Not to destroy—
but to uncover what's real beneath the rubble.

We're going to name some things. Unlearn others.
Ask questions not meant to shame—
but to free.

Because this isn't just about healing.
It's about remembering how to be human—
in the light of God's love.

You don't need to prove anything here.
You don't have to pretend you're not trembling.
You don't have to work harder to hold your soul together.
You are already being held.

And being held doesn't mean you won't shake—
It means you're not alone in the shaking.

So come.
With honesty.
With ache.
With your half-lit hope.

There's a fire already lit—
And a place at the table with your name on it.

You don't have to climb your way back to God.

He's already come looking for you.

CHAPTER ONE

When the Foundation Fails

❧ The Millennium Tower

The Millennium Tower in San Francisco
was meant to be a triumph of luxury and engineering.

Fifty-eight stories of glass and steel.
Luxury condos with panoramic views.

An architectural marvel—until it started to sink.

Then it started to lean.

Not because of a storm.
Not because of faulty materials.
But because the foundation wasn't
anchored to bedrock.

The building was beautiful.
But beneath the surface, it was failing.

Nobody noticed at first.
Everything looked fine on the outside.

But slowly—over years—
the tilt grew noticeable.

And with every inch, the danger deepened.
It's still standing.

Sometimes, the cracks aren't in buildings—they're in us.

❧ The Man in the Garage

He hadn't planned to sit in the garage that night.
Not for long, anyway.

But something about the stillness felt necessary.

No performance.
No pretending.
No one watching.

Just a man.
And a silence that had outlasted his striving.

The Bible beside him lay unopened.
The coffee was cold.
His boots were still on, though he hadn't moved in hours.

And when the words finally came, they weren't rehearsed.
They weren't shouted.
They weren't holy.

"I don't know who You are anymore."

They weren't angry.
They were tired.

Years of faithful effort.
Years of sincere belief.
Years of doing all the right things.

And still, the ache.
Still, the silence.
Still, the sense that something wasn't right.

He'd prayed before.
Wept before.
Rededicated before.

But the foundation—
the inner structure beneath his spiritual life—
was beginning to tilt.

He still believed in Jesus.
That wasn't the problem.

The problem was...
he no longer believed he could change.

He loved Christ.
But he didn't trust himself.

And though he couldn't have said it
in that moment,
something in him was beginning to break open:

The foundation he'd built his faith on
wasn't bedrock after all.

What do you do when you've built a life
on obedience, service, and faithfulness—
and still feel like the walls are
cracking?

Maybe…you don't need to tear it all down.
Maybe you just need to dig underneath it.

Not demolition.
Excavation.

See Matthew 7:24–27

❧ A Flicker of Light

That night in the garage,
the man picked up his old Bible.

Not out of duty.
But out of desperation.

He reached for his old friend.

It opened to John 1:

> *"In the beginning was the Word,*
> *and the Word was with God,*
> *and the Word was God…*
> *In Him was life,*
> *and that life was the light of men.*
> *The light shines in the darkness,*
> *and the darkness has not overcome it."*
> *— John 1:1–5*

He read it slowly.
Not to understand.
But to breathe.

And as the words settled over him,
a flicker stirred.

Not a resolution.
Not a breakthrough.

Just... a flicker.

A flicker of hope that maybe
this wasn't the end of his story.

That maybe the Light still finds the flickering.

That maybe...
he wasn't alone.

❧ An Old Promise

Another verse surfaced—unlooked for:

> *"A bruised reed He will not break,*
> *and a faintly burning wick He*
> *will not snuff out."*
> — *Isaiah 42:3*

That's what he was.
A faintly burning wick.

Not a blazing fire.
Not a strong torch.

Just a flicker.

But the Word said…
He wouldn't snuff it out.

So the man whispered—
barely loud enough to hear himself:

"I still trust You.
I just don't know how to be any
better than this."

There was no answer.
No flash of glory.
No warm presence.

Just a man.
And a Word.
And a flicker.

And maybe…that was enough.

❧ Reflection

- Where do you feel like the foundation of your faith has begun to shift or crack?

- Are there areas where you've tried everything you were taught… but still feel stuck or disconnected?

- Can you name the difference between what you were told faith would feel like…and what it actually feels like now?

❧ Practice

Light a candle and sit quietly for a few minutes.

Watch the flame flicker.
Let it remind you
that even a faint light
is not forgotten.

❧ Prayer

Jesus,

I don't have a script tonight.
I'm not trying to impress You.

I'm just tired of pretending the foundation feels solid
when it doesn't.

I still believe You.
I still want You.
But I don't know what comes next.

So I give You permission
to show me what's real.

If I need to unlearn,
help me unlearn.

If I need to dig,
help me dig.

✺ False Blueprints

Before he ever made a conscious choice,
the man had already learned what
love cost.

Long before he could name God,
he'd formed ideas about what
made someone acceptable,
what made someone safe,
and what made someone… leave.

It wasn't a single moment.
It was a million moments.

A look.
A rule.
A silence.
A punishment that echoed louder
than any apology.

This wasn't rebellion.
This was formation.

Not the kind that's chosen,
but the kind that's absorbed.

Somewhere along the line,
he started to believe
that the way to be close to God
was to stay out of His way.

To stay faithful.
To keep all the rules.

To not make noise.
To be good—
and maybe good would earn him love.

It wasn't written on stone tablets.
But it was etched into his soul all the same.
And the blueprint stuck.

You follow all the instructions.
You stay close to the lines.
You memorize the verses.
You confess what's wrong.
You attend the meetings.
You teach the class.
You smile when you're supposed to.

But deep down, you're still wondering:
Am I really wanted?
Or just tolerated because I'm useful?

That's the danger of transactional faith:

It gives you a sense of control…until you lose it.

And when it breaks, it tells you that
you are the one who failed.

But transformation is different.
Transformation doesn't come through bargains.
It comes through presence.

Jesus doesn't meet us where we perform.
He meets us where we're honest.

❧ Contracts of Belief

Long before the garage,
he had already signed them—
the silent contracts.

Not with a pen.
But with his soul.

Agreements like:

I am only as valuable as my behavior.
If I mess up, I must make up for it.
Love disappears when I disappoint.

Intentions don't matter—
only how others interpret me.

I am powerless to explain or defend
what I meant.

Misunderstanding is inevitable,
and dangerous.

They weren't reasoned to.
They were absorbed.

And once they took root,
they shaped everything.

Even God.
Especially God.

❧ The Voice We Trusted

It's often the voices we trust most
that shape us the deepest.

Sometimes they sound like fathers.
Sometimes like mothers, siblings, teachers, or church leaders.
Sometimes like a coach.
Sometimes like a childhood friend.
Sometimes it's not just what they said…
but what they didn't.

He could still hear his father's voice.
Not in anger.
But in statements that landed like bricks:

"You'll never amount to anything."
"Why do you keep messing up?"
"Can't you get anything right?"

They weren't shouted.
They were sighed.
Worn grooves in the house of his memory.

And the boy didn't just hear them.
He believed them.

He tried harder.
He got quieter.
He learned to perform.
He built on those words as if they
were blueprints.

He didn't know if he could take disappointment again.
Not again.

He'd learned to fear hope more than pain.
Pain was predictable.
Hope made promises.

But even as the fear rose...
something quieter was present.
Something unspoken.

It wasn't assurance.
Not yet.
But it was a kind of presence.

Gentle.
Unrushed.
Not asking for anything.

He didn't know if it was God.
But for the first time in a long time...
he didn't want to run.

A verse returned,
like an ember caught in the wind:

> "Where can I go from your Spirit?
> Where can I flee from your presence?
> If I go up to the heavens, you are there;
> if I make my bed in the depths, you are there.
> If I rise on the wings of the dawn,
> if I settle on the far side of the sea,
> even there your hand will guide me,
> your right hand will hold me fast."
> — Psalm 139:7–10

He didn't feel held.
But maybe…
just maybe…
he was.

❧ Reflection

Returning to the Foundation

Take a breath.
You don't have to fix anything right now.
You don't have to prove your
sincerity, or your worth, or your readiness.

You are already being seen.
And the Father is not disappointed
in your distance.
He's just glad you're still within sight.

Maybe you've been running.
Maybe you've been hiding.
Maybe you've been building on
someone else's blueprint your whole life.

That's okay.

You're not too far gone to return.
You're not too broken to rebuild.
And you're not too late to be loved.

You are already loved.
Before the apology.

Before the correction.
Before the cleanup.

You. Are. Loved.

Being loved doesn't erase the ache,
but it anchors you in the truth
that you are never abandoned.

❧ Let These Questions Guide Your Quiet

- What contracts of belief did I unknowingly sign about love, value, or acceptance?

- How have those false blueprints shaped how I see God—and how I believe He sees me?

- Am I ready to let Jesus rewrite those contracts with love?

❧ Practice

Write out one "contract of belief"
you want to break.
Then physically tear up the paper
as a symbol of release.

If you're not ready to let go, that's okay.
Just notice what comes up as you
sit with these questions.

If you feel led, share one of these "contracts" or insights
with a trusted friend, spiritual director, or counselor.

❧ Prayer of Freedom

Coming Out of Agreement with the Lie

Father,

You see the places in me that have gone quiet.
The places I've covered, or lost, or buried.

Thank You for not turning away.
Thank You for still running.

Help me unlearn what fear has taught me.
Help me believe You're not ashamed of me.
Help me trust that I am loved—
not eventually, but now.

In Jesus' name,

I come out of agreement with the lie
that I am only as loved as I am useful.
I break the contract that says I must
earn Your affection.

These voices no longer have authority in my life.

I don't have all the words.
But I want You more than I want answers.

If there's a way back to love…

I'm ready to take the first step.

Amen.

The Only Foundation
Strong Enough

You can only push for so long.
Only carry the weight for so many years.

Eventually, even the most devout
among us begin to crack—
not because we stopped believing,
but because we were never taught
what to believe about God's love.

Most of us were handed a spiritual blueprint
built on effort, guilt, and fear.
We were formed by performance,
rewarded for pretending, and told to
try harder when we were breaking.

And when it didn't hold, we
assumed it was our fault.
But what if the foundation itself was flawed?

What if all your striving wasn't proof
that you're failing—but proof that
you're building on something that
was never meant to bear the weight
of your soul?

Maybe what's been missing all
along isn't more discipline, more
insight, or more repentance.

Maybe what's missing is what was
always meant to be there first:

Love.

Not the abstract kind.
Not the polite kind.
Not the kind that smiles from a
distance while you collapse inside.

But the fierce, faithful, personal love
of God that sees all of you—
and stays.

Before we go any further,
before we talk about healing,
discipleship, obedience, calling, or
transformation…
we have to stop.

And go back.

Back to the beginning.
Back to what we were made for.
Back to the only place strong
enough to build a life:

The love of God.

CHAPTER THREE

The Love That Rebuilds

There's a place most Christians
don't talk about.
Not from pulpits.
Not at men's groups.
Not even in the quiet of their own souls.

It's the dark side of the moon.

On the light side, life appears mostly good.
You orbit where everyone can see you—
upright, disciplined, mostly clean.

You show up.
You pray when you're supposed to.
You read your Bible, go to church,
volunteer when it's asked of you.
You keep your struggles to yourself.
You try to look like someone who
knows what he's doing—even if you don't.
You shake hands, smile at the door,
keep your secrets tucked beneath your Sunday shirt.

And for a while, it works.
You keep your orbit in the light—
at least on the outside.
And as long as you do, you can
almost believe that God loves you.
You assume He sees you. You
assume He's near.
You feel… tolerable.

But every moon has a far side—
a shadowed hemisphere no one else sees.

And then it happens.
You fail.
You compromise.
You cross a line no one else notices,
but you feel it crack through your soul.

Suddenly, you're spun out of the
light, drifting into shadow.
The dark side.

Where shame whispers louder than Scripture.
Where God feels silent, and prayer feels foolish.
Where you believe you've wandered
too far, failed too deeply,
disappointed too many times.

You sit in the dim glow of your
phone, scrolling past verses you can't feel.
The silence in your chest is heavier
than the night outside your window.
You wait in the shadow,

as if enough time in darkness might somehow
earn you a way back to the light.

And then the old rhythm begins:

Shame → guilt → confession → resolution → trying harder → falling
again → hiding → shame.

Orbiting between light and
darkness, but never landing in love.

It's not because you don't believe in God.
It's not because you don't want Him.
It's because, deep down—under all
your doctrine and spiritual effort—
you were never taught how to
actually receive His love.

You believe God loves people.
You might even believe God loves
you… generally.
But not here.
Not now.
Not on this side of the moon.

If you recognize yourself here,
you're not alone.
You're not broken beyond repair.
You've just never truly understood
what His love is.
Or how far it goes.
Or how deeply, personally,
relentlessly His love pursues you.

But here's the truth:

That story you've been living?
That cycle you've come to accept as normal?
That quiet belief that God's love
stops when your failure starts?

That's just not the truth.

And when we finally know the truth—
the real truth about who God is and
how He loves us—
we will be set free.

See John 8:32

So let's go find out.
Let's walk together into what is
more true than your shame,
more solid than your performance,
stronger than your resolve,
and nearer than you dared to believe.

His love is not a reward for the worthy,
but a rescue for the lost.
It doesn't wait for you in the light—
it walks with you through the dark.
It doesn't flicker when you fail.
It shines on both sides of the moon.

It's time to set the story straight—
not just about you,
but about Him.

Even on the far side of the moon,
you are not beyond the reach of
Love.

"God's love is the bedrock.
Every trauma, every lie, every
wandering is a crack from forgetting that.
To rebuild, we don't just correct beliefs—
we return to the One who calls us Beloved."
　　　　—Paul Jones

"There is nothing you can do to
make God love you more;
there is nothing you can do to
make God love you less."
　　　　— Philip Yancey

❧ There Are Words We Hear in Church

But rarely believe in the shadows.
Words that sound beautiful on the surface,
but feel impossible when you're
sitting in the dark—
when shame is louder than hope,
and God feels far away.

Most of us have been told that
God's love is unconditional.
But if we're honest, we wonder if
there's a limit—
some hidden line we can cross,
some place we can fall where love
won't follow.

We imagine God waiting for us to
get it together,
to climb back into the light,
to prove we're worth loving again.

But the truth is deeper, wilder, and
more relentless than we ever dared to hope.

> *"Where can I go from your Spirit?*
> *Where can I flee from your presence?*
> *If I go up to the heavens, you are there;*
> *if I make my bed in the depths, you are there.*
> *If I rise on the wings of the dawn,*
> *if I settle on the far side of the sea,*
> *even there your hand will guide me,*
> *your right hand will hold me fast."*
> — *Psalm 139:7–10*

Even on the far side of the moon,
even in the places we think are
beyond reach,
God's love is already there.
Not waiting for us to find our way back,
but holding us—right where we are.

This is the love that changes everything.
Not a theory.
Not a feeling.
Not a reward for the worthy.
But a presence that refuses to let go.

As you read this chapter, don't just
settle for knowing about God's love.

Let yourself be found by it.
Let yourself be held.

❧ A Holy Undoing

Somewhere along the way, most of
us were handed a version of God's
love that came with a catch.

Maybe it wasn't stated outright.
Maybe it was taught in the pauses,
in the sideways glances,
in the exhausted tone of a leader
or parent who meant well.

But the message was clear:

God loves you…
but you'd better not mess it up.

And so we tried.
Tried to be good.
Tried to stay clean.
Tried to pray enough,
care enough, perform enough.

Not because we didn't believe in God—
but because, deep down, we didn't
really believe He liked us.

So let's name it now.
Let's excavate it.

Let's pull out the rusted nails we
once called truth and ask the harder question:

What if the version of God's love
you were handed… wasn't love at all?

❧ What Love Was Never Meant to Be

Love is not the same thing as tolerance.
It's not appeasement or cold calculation.
It's not a reward.

But many of us were handed transactional faith:

If I obey, I'm loved.
If I worship, I'm welcome.
If I'm useful, I'm accepted.
If I fail, I'm forgotten.

And the heartbreaking part?
We thought it was true because it
felt true in human relationships—
parents, pastors, friends, even ourselves.

But God's love does not operate like ours.
It's not fueled by your faithfulness.
It's not triggered by your goodness.
It's not canceled by your failure.

> *"While we were still sinners,*
> *Christ died for us."*
> — *Romans 5:8*

His love goes first.
Before your improvement.
Before your confession.
Before your belief.
Before you even turned His direction—He called you beloved.

❧ When the Gospel Got Twisted

*"God's desire for intimacy with
you is the core of your identity."*
— *Tyler Staton, Praying Like Monks, Living Like Fools*

If intimacy is the core,
then distance is the disease.

Somewhere along the line, the
gospel got rearranged.
We heard about grace—but it
sounded like a transaction.
We heard about forgiveness—but it
felt like probation.
We heard that God was love—but
only if we behaved.

What we ended up with wasn't the gospel.
It was something else.
A yo-yo gospel.
A "God is near… until you fail."
A "He loves you… but is mostly disappointed"
kind of message.

And if we're honest, that belief
shaped us far more than we realized.
We built our identity not on the Rock—
but on the performance of the moment.
No wonder we've been exhausted.

❧ The Lies We Must Lay Down

It's time to name the old
architecture that cracked under pressure—
and replace it with truth:

The Lie: I must prove my worth

The Truth: I was chosen in love before I did anything

The Lie: I am only loved when I'm doing well

The Truth: His love doesn't fluctuate with my faithfulness

The Lie: God uses me, but He doesn't enjoy me

The Truth: He delights in me, even in my weakness

The Lie: If I mess up, I lose Him

The Truth: Nothing can separate me from His love (Romans 8:38–39)

❧ The Beloved Before the Beginning

> *"This is My beloved Son, in*
> *whom I am well pleased."*
> *— Matthew 3:17*

And Jesus hadn't healed anyone yet.
Hadn't preached a sermon.
Hadn't multiplied a single loaf of bread.
He had done nothing—except be the Son.
And the Father was already pleased.

Let that settle.

What if the voice that spoke over
Jesus… is speaking over you?
Not because you've done enough.
But because He already chose to love you.

> *"He chose us in Him before the*
> *foundation of the world… In love,*
> *He predestined us for adoption…"*
> — *Ephesians 1:4–5*

Before the failure.
Before the striving.
Before the mask.
He said: Mine.

✵ Identity Isn't Earned

You don't become the beloved through effort.
You realize it through encounter.

> *"Becoming the beloved means*
> *letting the truth of our*
> *belovedness become enfleshed*
> *in everything we think, say, or do."*
> — *Henri Nouwen, Life of the Beloved*

You don't need to achieve a new identity.
You need to receive it.

❧ Reflection for the Reader

- What lie has been hardest for you to let go of?

- What truth about God's love feels hardest to believe?

- Where do you sense the Spirit inviting you to rest, not strive?

❧ Reflection

The Light That Finds You

There is a kind of love that does not flinch.
It doesn't wince at your wounds or
grow weary of your need.
It is not fragile.
It is not afraid of your darkness.
It moves toward you when others pull away.
It holds steady when your faith cannot.
It stays.

This love is not earned.
It is not measured by your devotion
or performance.
It is older than your failure and
deeper than your shame.
It is not a reaction.
It is the beginning.

This love speaks into the silence,
shines into the shadow,
and whispers in your own voice:

"I have loved you with an
everlasting love."
(Even here. Even now. Even still.)

❧ Practice

Try sitting in silence for five minutes,
simply asking God to show you
where His love is already present—
even in your darkness.

If you're able, write down what
you notice or sense.

If you're not ready to let yourself be loved,
just notice what comes up as
you sit with these questions.

If you feel led, share what you
discover with a trusted friend,
spiritual director, or counselor.

❧ Prayer

Let Me Be Loved

God of light,
I am tired of hiding.

Tired of trying.
Tired of wearing masks in places
that should be safe.

I bring You not my best face,
but my real one.
The one with scars and failures and questions.
The one that fears Your silence
more than Your judgment.
The one that wants to believe You
love me—even here.

Let me feel Your presence in this shadowed place.
Let Your light expose not just my sin, but my worth.
Let Your love be louder than my shame.

I don't want to orbit anymore.
I want to land.
I want to be loved.
Really loved.
By You.

I know now:

You don't wait for me in the light
You come for me in the dark.

So here I am.
Found.
Held.
Yours.

Amen.

✺ Alternate Prayer

A Prayer for the Beloved

Father,

I have lived by lies that said Your love was earned,
that I had to climb my way back to You,
that I was only as welcome as I was worthy.

But today I want to believe what's true—
that Your love finds me,
even on the far side of the moon.
That You are not waiting for me to get it right,
but holding me in the dark,
calling me Beloved before I ever
called You Lord.

Help me lay down the old contracts.
Help me rest in the truth that I am Yours,
not because I am good,
but because You are.

Let Your love rebuild what shame tried to destroy.
Let me receive what I could never earn.
And let me live, today, as one who is already held.

Amen.

CHAPTER FOUR

The Yo-Yo Gospel

When Formation Replaces Foundation

❧ Author's Note

This chapter explores how deeply our identity is shaped by the words spoken to us—especially in childhood. If parts of this feel tender, that's okay. You're not reading alone. The One who sees everything you carry is already here, reading with you. And His voice is stronger than every one that ever wounded you.

❧ The Echo

There's an old playground chant
we all heard at some point:
"Sticks and stones may break my bones,
but words will never hurt me."
We said it with bravado.
We were trying to be tough.

But it wasn't true.
Bones heal.
Words settle.
They don't just bruise.

They build—or break.
They shape the framework of how we see the world,
and more deeply… how we see ourselves.

❧ The Voice We Trusted

He could still hear it.
His father's voice not loud, not cruel,
but cutting all the same:
"Why do you keep messing up?"
"Can't you get anything right?"
"You'll never amount to anything."

They were just words.
But they landed like laws.
He didn't rebel. He tried harder.
He worked for approval like it was oxygen.

And somewhere along the line,
he built his identity around those echoes.
That's how soul contracts are signed—
not with pens, but with pain.

And for some, those words didn't come from a father.
They came from a mother.
A sibling.
A teacher.
A bully.
Even a pastor.

But they all left the same imprint:
You are only as loved as you are useful.

"We come into the world looking
for someone looking for us.
And we remain in the world hoping
to find someone who never looked away."
　　　　　— Dr. Curt Thompson, The Soul of Shame

But when that gaze is absent...
when the words that should have named us
instead condemned us...
we carry the ache of being unseen
into every future place we try to belong.

❧ Formation Without Foundation

Long before the man ended up in the garage—
knees on concrete, whispering
toward the silence—
he had already begun building a life
on shifting ground.
He didn't know it, of course.
No one does when they're three or four.

But somewhere in those early years,
a message was etched into his inner world—
not in words, but in feelings.
Moments of innocent joy were sometimes
met not with safety,
but correction.

Expressions of freedom or delight
were misunderstood,
even punished.

The lesson landed quietly:
Stay small.
Stay safe.
Stay in line.

It wasn't cruelty. It was formation—
shaped by love that was trying to protect,
trying to provide,
trying to manage more than any
heart was built to hold.

But here's the deeper truth—
the one most of us never name:
Those early relationships—
especially with our parents—often
become the blueprint for
how we understand God.

When love felt conditional,
we assumed God's love was too.

When affection was tied to performance,
we carried that expectation into our spiritual life.

When correction came more quickly than compassion,
we began to brace ourselves for
God's disappointment rather than run to Him in weakness.

❧ The Gospel Beneath the Gospel

So by the time we met Christ—
truly, personally—

we were already carrying assumptions
about what He must be like.

He loved us, yes.
But He was also watching.
Measuring.
Waiting.

And so began the gospel we would
live by for decades:
Try harder.
Stay in control.
Don't disappoint.

And if you mess up,
brace for distance.

But that wasn't the real gospel.

It was a gospel beneath the gospel—
a yo-yo theology of closeness and withdrawal,
faith and failure,
striving and shame.

We knew Jesus saved us.
But we weren't sure He liked us.

❧ Soul Contracts

Foundations aren't changed
by hindsight alone.
They are changed when hindsight
becomes awareness—

when we begin to name what we
didn't know we were believing.

This is the excavation.
And when the man looked closely,
he saw them—
those old soul contracts,
still shaping how he saw everything.

They weren't just thoughts.
They were agreements.

Things like:

- If I disappoint someone, love might disappear.

- If I'm misunderstood, I must be dangerous.

- If I speak up, I might be punished.

- If I'm not useful, I don't belong.

- If I cry, I'm weak.

- If I succeed, maybe I'll be safe.

He never chose them consciously.
They were formed in survival.

And then reinforced through religion.

He memorized verses.
Led worship.
Served others.
Shared the gospel.

Tried to forgive.
Tried to be holy.
Tried to be enough.
But it never felt settled.

The joy of the Lord always seemed
just out of reach.
Not because it wasn't real…
but because he didn't know how to receive it.
He kept looking for the formula.

Kept thinking there must be a better system—
some combination of steps or submission
that would finally unlock the wholeness
everyone else seemed to have.
But under all that striving…
there was a Voice.

Calling.
Present.
Patient.

And though he couldn't name it yet,
that Voice was whispering:
"You are not what was spoken over you.

You are who I say you are.
And I never left you."

❧ Scripture Echoes

He remembered a passage.
One he had heard a hundred times,
but never like this:

> *"The Lord your God is with you,*
> *He is mighty to save.*
> *He will take great delight in you;*
> *He will quiet you with his love,*
> *He will rejoice over you with singing."*
>   — *Zephaniah 3:17*

Could that be real?
Could God actually… delight?
Could God sing?

And could He really be with him?
Even now?

❧ Reflection

- What Was Spoken, What are the earliest words I remember shaping how I saw myself?

- Were there any phrases I heard that I now realize became part of my identity?

- What would it mean to let Jesus speak a better word over me?

❧ Practice

Take a few minutes to write down
one phrase or belief from your past
that still echoes in your mind.

Then, write a new phrase beside it—
something you sense Jesus might
say to you instead.
If you feel comfortable, share this
with a trusted friend or simply sit quietly,
letting the better word settle in.

❧ Prayer

Breaking the Soundtrack

Jesus,

I have been living by words that
were never Yours.

Some I heard once.
Some I heard for years.
Some I told myself.

They sound like protection.
But they've become a prison.

You are the Word.
You are the Voice I was made to hear.
And You are not ashamed to speak to me now.

So I come out of agreement with
every false word spoken over me.

I break the contract with condemnation.
I reject the voice of shame.

And I welcome Your voice instead.

Speak, Lord.

I am listening.
And I want to believe what You say...
even if it takes time to believe it all
the way through.

CHAPTER FIVE

The Gaze That Heals

Seeing, and Being Seen, in the Light of Love

❧ Author's Note

This chapter gently explores what it means to be truly seen by God—and how our vision, shaped by pain or fear, often distorts what is already true. If you've ever struggled to believe you're lovable, especially when no one is looking, this chapter is for you. The eyes of Christ do not flinch. And neither does His love.

❧ When No One Was Watching

He didn't say it out loud.
He hadn't said much of anything for a while.

But the ache had been there since he was a boy.
It wasn't rebellion.
It was fatigue.

A kind of soul-exhaustion that
doesn't show up in words,
but in withdrawal.

He had grown used to performing—
at church, at work, with friends, even with God.
But something had shifted.

He wasn't angry. He was tired.
The kind of tired that doesn't come from doing too much…
but from being unseen for too long.

It was strange, really.
He knew the Scriptures.
He knew God loved him.
But he didn't feel it.

❧ The Invisible Ache

There's a pain that comes from
being ignored.
From being misread.
From being seen—but not known.

It's subtle.
But it shapes everything.

It makes you doubt your motives.
It makes you second-guess your worth.
It makes you wonder if you'll ever be enough—
or if you've already been
disqualified and no one had the
heart to tell you.

He carried that pain quietly.
Years of being the good son.

The faithful volunteer.
The one who always showed up,
even when it hurt.

But there was no applause in the silence.
No hand on the shoulder.
No voice saying, "I see you."

He didn't need a stage.
He just needed to feel real.
But somewhere along the line,
he stopped believing that was possible.

❧ The Glance That Doesn't Look Away

And then one day—unexpectedly—
he remembered a story.
Not a sermon.
A moment.

Peter, after the rooster crowed.
After the denial.
After the promise had been broken
and shame began to settle.

Luke's Gospel says:

> *"The Lord turned and looked straight at Peter."*
> *— Luke 22:61*

No words.
Just a look.

The kind of look that pierces.
The kind of look that doesn't flinch.

And for some reason, that verse
stayed with him.

Jesus looked at Peter—not with rage,
but with recognition.
Not with rejection,
but with remembrance.

Peter had failed.
Jesus had not.
And still… He looked.

❧ The Fear of Being Seen

He had always feared that moment—
the moment of being fully known.

He'd imagined that if God really saw him,
He'd turn away.
He imagined disgust.
Disappointment.
A sigh. A shake of the head.

But the longer he sat with that story,
the more he wondered…

What if Jesus never looked away?
What if He looked and kept looking?
What if His gaze was not a

searchlight for sin—
but a spotlight on belovedness?

❧ The Eye That Doesn't Condemn

He remembered another story.
A woman caught in adultery.
Dragged into public shame.
Surrounded by accusers.

And Jesus…stoops.
Writes in the dirt.
Waits.

Then looks up and says:

> *"Let the one without sin throw the first stone."*
> *—John 8:7*

And slowly… they all walk away.

Then He speaks again:

> *"Woman, where are they?*
> *Has no one condemned you?"*
> *"No one, Lord."*
> *"Then neither do I condemn you."*
> *—John 8:10–11*

And He looks at her—really looks.
Not as property.
Not as failure.
Not as cautionary tale.

But as daughter.
Image-bearer.
Beloved.

❧ The Light That Stays

There is a kind of seeing that heals.
Not the kind that scrutinizes.
The kind that stays.

That sees the trembling parts and doesn't flinch.
That knows the wound and isn't
afraid of the blood.
That hears the silence beneath the words
and speaks peace into the ache.

That is how Jesus sees.

❧ The Story He Never Forgot

He remembered something else.
Another fire. Another glance.
Another story of a man who failed—
and a Savior who stayed.

> *"When they landed, they saw a charcoal fire in place..."*
> *— John 21:9*

Jesus, risen from the dead,
had made breakfast.

A fire.
Some fish.
Some bread.

And Peter—who had failed spectacularly—
was invited not to explain himself,
but to eat.

And to answer a question.
Not "Why did you fail?"
But:
"Do you love Me?"

Three denials.
Three questions.
Three answers.
And a commission.
"Feed My sheep."

The look hadn't changed.
But the moment had.
The fire that once seared with shame
now smelled like restoration.

❧ Curt Thompson writes:

"The gaze of God is not a
judging stare...
it is the loving attention of the
One who delights in seeing us.
When we allow ourselves to be
seen, shame begins to lose its grip."

He read that quote slowly.
Then again.

And something deep in him stirred.

Maybe this was the turning point.
Maybe healing wasn't found in more doing…
but in being seen,
and not rejected.

❧ Reflection

Seen and Safe

- When did I first feel unseen or misunderstood in a way that shaped how I see myself?
- How has shame shaped the way I imagine God sees me?
- What would it mean to sit by the fire of my past and let Jesus look at me with love?

❧ Prayer

For the One Who Longs to Be Seen

Jesus,

I've been afraid to be seen—
not by people,
but by You.

I've imagined Your eyes as flames,
not kindness.
I've braced for punishment,
even when You offered peace.

But I want to believe what is true.
I want to sit by the fire.
I want to hear Your question,
and not run from the answer.

You are not ashamed of me.
You are not tired of looking.

So here I am.
Seen.
And still loved.

Stay with me here.
Speak what I'm ready to hear.
And lead me gently forward.

Amen.

CHAPTER SIX

The Way of Love Begins Here

❧ Author's Note

Many of us have known the ache of spiritual weariness—the slow erosion of a faith built on shaky ground. This isn't mystical silence or holy desolation. It's confusion. Disillusionment. The gradual collapse of beliefs that never quite fit.

Some of us grew up believing that
God was angry—waiting for us to
mess up. We learned a gospel of sin management rather than soul transformation. We missed the
heart of the story: that love actually means love.

But then something shifts. We begin
to hear a different tone in God's
voice. We start to see a Father who
runs to meet His children. We
discover that transformation begins with truth, not willpower—with letting God love us first.

This chapter begins that journey of re-forming. Not with another system, but with the gentle work of rebuilding on solid ground.

❧ The Way of Love Begins Here

He reached for his Bible—not from
guilt or duty, but from genuine
desire.

For the first time in years, the pages didn't feel heavy.
He wasn't searching for a fix or a command to obey.
He just wanted to listen.

He let his eyes linger over the
words, not rushing, not striving.
The phrases seemed to breathe—
less like demands, more like
invitations.

A particular passage caught his attention—
one he'd read before but never truly heard:

> *"The LORD, the LORD, a God merciful and gracious, slow to
> anger, and abounding in steadfast love and faithfulness…"*
> *— Exodus 34:6, ESV*

He paused.
Read it again.
Slowly.

That's how God describes Himself.
Not first and foremost as Judge.
But as merciful. Gracious. Steady.

The words settled into places that
had been braced for

disappointment.
This wasn't the God of his
childhood fears.
This was Someone else entirely.

He realized he wasn't reading
to get through a chapter.
He was letting the chapter get
through to him.

A quiet joy flickered—tentative,
unfamiliar, but real.
He found himself soaking in the
words, letting them seep into places
that had been dry for years.

He didn't need to understand everything.
He just needed to be present.

For the first time, Scripture felt less
like a test and more like a table—
a place to sit, to be nourished, to
belong.

He closed the Bible and sat back,
letting the moment linger.
He felt no urge to move on,
no pressure to "do" anything next.
Just a gentle fullness,
like the hush after rain.

❧ The Unexpected Call

The phone rang, startling him out of his reverie.
He glanced at the screen—a familiar name.
A mentor. Someone who had walked with him through other seasons,
who had seen both his striving and his silence.

He answered, voice still soft from
the quiet.

> *"Hey. You've been on my mind," the mentor said.*
> *"I don't know why, but I felt like I should check in.*
> *How are you, really?"*

They talked for a few minutes,
nothing urgent or profound—just a
real conversation.
A question.
A listening ear.
An invitation:

"Let's grab coffee this week. I'd love to see you."

When the call ended,
he sat for a moment, phone in hand,
feeling the warmth of being remembered.

It wasn't a sermon or a solution.
Just a soft touch of love—an
answer to a prayer he hadn't quite
put into words.

❧ Small Beginnings

He realized, with a quiet sense of
awe, that maybe this is how the Kingdom grows:
not with fanfare, but with small,
hidden beginnings.

A seed in the soil.
A word that lands and lingers.
A call from a friend.

He remembered Jesus' words:

> *"The kingdom of God is like a mustard seed, which a man took
> and planted in his field. Though
> it is the smallest of all seeds, yet
> when it grows, it is the largest of
> garden plants and becomes a
> tree, so that the birds come and
> perch in its branches."*
> — *Matthew 13:31–32*

He smiled, realizing that today was
not a breakthrough,
but a beginning.
A seed, planted and watered—
quiet, unseen, but alive.

This is the way of re-forming.
Not through force or formula.
But through the gentle
accumulation of grace.
Small kindnesses.

Quiet moments.
The steady work of love rebuilding
what fear had broken.

❧ Learning a New Rhythm

He thought about something he'd
read recently—words that had
stayed with him:

> *"The greatest thing we can do*
> *in life is to learn to live as Jesus*
> *would live if He were us."*
> — *Dallas Willard*

Not by trying harder.
But by learning the rhythm of grace.
By letting transformation begin
with truth, not willpower.
By discovering that love—real love—
was enough to start over.

This wasn't about managing
behavior to keep God close.
It was about learning to receive
the presence of the One who never left.

❧ Reflection for the Reader

- Where have you experienced the Kingdom as a seed—small, quiet, but real?
- What does it feel like to be remembered, to be invited, to be loved in the ordinary?
- How might you let today's small grace take root, without rushing it to grow?

❧ Practice

Pause for a moment of stillness.
Let yourself recall a recent "small grace"—
a gentle word, a quiet
invitation, a moment of being remembered.

Write it down, and thank God for it.
Ask Him to help you notice and
nurture these seeds of love as they appear.

❧ A Prayer for Small Beginnings

Father,

Thank You for the quiet ways
Your Kingdom comes—in words
that nourish, in friends who
remember, in the slow growth I
cannot force.

Help me trust the seed,
to welcome the gentle beginnings,

and to believe that what starts in
stillness will one day bear fruit.

Let me be present to Your love,
and open to the invitations You
send—
even when they arrive as softly as a
phone call or a verse that lingers.

Amen.

❧ Before You Begin

The First Question

And perhaps before you begin, you should know this:

The very first words Jesus speaks
in the Gospel of John were not a command or a sermon.
They were a question.

Two disciples followed Him—
tentative, curious, unsure.
He turned, saw them coming,
and simply asked:

> *"What do you seek?"*
> —*John 1:38, ESV*

But in Greek, the question is deeper:

τί ζητεῖτε — What do you long for?

He didn't ask what they knew.
Or what they believed.
He asked what they desired.

And He's still asking.
Not with pressure.
Not with judgment.
But with open eyes, open arms, and
a table already set.

What do you long for?

Let that be the question you carry
with you into the next chapter.

CHAPTER SEVEN

Walking in the Quiet—Transformation in Process

The Morning Awakening

He stood at the window, coffee in
hand, watching the morning fog
drift past.

The mug was warm, grounding him
in the present.

Outside, a gentle breeze stirred the
leaves, setting them to whisper and dance.

A single bird called—a thin,
persistent note—soon joined by
others, their songs weaving through
the quiet air.

He wondered how many mornings
he'd missed these simple, beautiful moments,
just to rush into the day—
never noticing the world waking up around him.

He let his gaze linger.

The leaves seemed to wave in
greeting, moved by the invisible
hand of the Spirit still stirring upon
the earth.
The birds sang as if creation itself
was offering praise, their voices
rising in a chorus older than
memory.

For the first time, he felt truly awake—
not just to the world, but to the
God who made it.

It was a small awakening, but it was real.
He realized that even in the
ordinary, the sacred was waiting to
be seen.

❧ Grace

The Cornerstone of Transformation

There is a reason the journey is
slow, and the reason is grace.

Grace is not just a word we recite in church. In the Bible, grace is deep,
rich, and surprising—sometimes translated from Hebrew (ḥēn, ḥesed),
Greek (charis), or Aramaic (ṭībūtā).

It's more than kindness; it's a royal invitation, a gift that changes you,
the very flavor of God's own nature.

In the Ancient Near East, favor or
grace was a relational, covenantal act.
A king would extend ḥēn to someone unworthy—a display of royal
generosity that required both humility and trust.
It was personal, not abstract.

In first-century Greco-Roman culture, charis referred to the benefaction
system. A wealthy patron gave a gift (charis) to someone in need, and
the proper response was not repayment, but gratitude (eucharistia) and
loyalty.
Paul redeems this idea, showing God as the generous Patron and us as
unworthy recipients of divine favor.

Jesus, speaking Aramaic, likely used words derived from ṭab—
meaning "good" or "beautiful."
Grace, then, was the outflowing of
God's tov nature—His goodness
finding you, not you finding it.

Scripture says:

> *"For it is by grace you have been saved,*
> *through faith—and this is not from yourselves,*
> *it is the gift of God—not by works,*
> *so that no one can boast."*
> — *Ephesians 2:8–9*

Grace is not only the starting point
of salvation; it is the ongoing power
that sustains every step of our
journey.

Paul writes:

> *"We have gained access by faith into this*
> *grace in which we now stand."*
> *— Romans 5:2*

Grace is the gentle strength that
carries us when we falter, the quiet invitation to begin again, and the
assurance that we are never alone
in our transformation.

Eugene Peterson put it simply:

> *"Grace is the air we breathe."*

Philip Yancey reminds us:

> *"Grace means there is nothing*
> *we can do to make God love us more, and nothing we can do to make*
> *Him love us less."*
> *— Philip Yancey, What's So Amazing About Grace?*

Paul Jones observes:

> *"Grace isn't God letting us off the hook—*
> *it's Him lifting us onto*
> *His shoulders. Grace is costly.*
> *It flows from the wounds of Christ*
> *and fills the cracks in us.*
> *It's not just forgiveness; it's formation.*
> *It is the voice of the Father calling us*
> *'beloved' before we ever prove anything."*

As Dallas Willard writes:

> *"Grace is not opposed to effort,*
> *but to earning. It is the action of*
> *God at work in your soul to do*
> *what you cannot do alone."*
> — Dallas Willard, *The Great Omission*

Grace is not a license to remain unchanged, but the very power by which change becomes possible.

It is the love of God poured into our hearts, freeing us from shame and striving, and inviting us to rest in His sufficiency.

❧ Understanding Grace

Grace Is:

- God's unearned favor and empowering presence
- Rooted in covenantal loyalty and love
- A person—Jesus, who finds us before we find Him
- The divine power to become who God sees you to be

Grace Is Not:

- A license to keep sinning
- Cold judicial pardon
- A mere doctrinal concept
- Passive kindness or indulgence

❧ Pause & Receive

Where do you need this kind of
grace today?

Can you let yourself be found, lifted,
and called "beloved"—even before
you prove anything?

Grace is the cornerstone.
Without it, transformation is
impossible.
With it, even our slowest progress is precious to God.

❧ Grace in the Story of God

- Genesis: Noah "found grace in the eyes of the LORD" (Genesis 6:8)

- Exodus: Moses pleads, "If I have found grace in your eyes…" (Exodus 33:13)

- John 1: Grace becomes incarnate

- Revelation 22:21: "The grace of the Lord Jesus be with all." Grace is the final word

❧ Poetic Reflection

The Grace That Finds

It found you
before you knew
you were lost.

It sang
while you were silencing hope,
and it waited
while you fought to earn it.

Grace does not knock—
it walks in through
the torn veil
and sits beside you
until you remember
you are already home.

❧ The Reader's Journey

The Slow Work of Grace

Maybe you know this quiet, too.
Not the silence of abandonment,
but the hush that comes when
striving fades.

Transformation, as Jesus described
it, is rarely sudden.
The Kingdom grows like a seed—
hidden, slow, persistent.

Matthew 13:31–32

We live in a world obsessed with
quick fixes and instant results.
But the way of Jesus is different.

It's about abiding, not achieving.
Resting, not rushing.

Scripture reminds us:

> *"Be still, and know that I am God."*
> — *Psalm 46:10*

> *"Abide in my love."*
> — *John 15:9*

Real change happens beneath the surface, often unnoticed.
It's in the pause before a harsh
word, the gentle response that
surprises even you, the growing awareness that you are not alone—
even in the fog.

❧ Pause & Breathe

Take a moment.
Set the book down if you need to.
Let your breath settle.

Notice the sounds around you—
the hum of the house,
the world outside your window,
the faint aroma of coffee,
the feel of sunlight on your skin.

Let yourself be here, now,
without rushing to the next thing.

❧ Why Transformation Feels Slow

As you linger in the quiet,
you may wonder why change takes so long.

Spiritual formation is not a self-improvement project.
It's the process of becoming more
like Christ—slowly, honestly, and
with much grace.

Ruth Haley Barton writes:

> *"Transformation is a long obedience in the same direction.
> It is not a quick fix, but a slow and
> steady turning of the heart toward God."*
>   *— Ruth Haley Barton, Sacred Rhythms*

Henri Nouwen reminds us:

> *"Solitude is the furnace of transformation. In the lonely place,
> we meet not only ourselves, but God."*
>   *— Henri Nouwen, The Way of the Heart*

Aundi Kolber encourages:

> *"Try softer. The invitation of God
> is not to push harder, but to yield to
> the gentle work of the Spirit within."*
>   *— Aundi Kolber, Try Softer*

Like the slow unfolding of dawn, or
the patient growth of roots beneath
the soil, God's work in us is often
hidden but always real.

❧ Lectio Divina Practice

Let's try something ancient and simple.

Choose one of these scriptures:

- "Abide in my love." (John 15:9)
- "Be still, and know that I am God." (Psalm 46:10)
- "My grace is sufficient for you, for my power is made perfect in weakness." (2 Corinthians 12:9)

Read it slowly.
Let each word rest on your heart.
Read it again, even slower.

What word or phrase stands out?
Let it echo.
Sit with it in silence for a minute or two.

Ask God to speak—not in thunder,
but in the quiet.

❧ The Heart of the Matter

There's an old saying:

You can't change the way you live
until you change the way you think.

But I've learned something deeper:

You can't change the way you think
until you understand the way you believe.

And belief always begins in the heart.
Jesus said:

> *"Out of the abundance of the heart the mouth speaks."*
> *— Matthew 12:34, ESV*

If you want to see lasting change,
don't start with your behavior.
Start with your heart—what you
truly believe about God, about yourself, about love.

Brennan Manning once wrote:

> *"Define yourself radically as one beloved by God.*
> *This is the true self. Every other identity is illusion."*
> *— Brennan Manning, Abba's Child*

Let that sink in: beloved.

Not productive.
Not impressive.
Beloved.

❧ Pause & Reflect

What do you believe—deep down—
about God's love for you?

Where do you notice slow,
subtle changes in your words or actions?

How do you experience God's
presence in the quiet or the fog?

What would it look like to "abide" in love,
even when you can't see the
next step?

Can you recall a moment when
grace surprised you—when you felt accepted,
forgiven, or simply loved,
even when you least expected it?

Write a few lines in the margin, or
just let the questions linger in your
heart.

❧ The Fog Is Not Failure

Some days, the fog lingers.
You may feel lonely, uncertain,
or wonder if you're making any
progress at all.

But the presence of God is not
measured by your emotions.
He is with you in the quiet, working
in ways you cannot always see.

Barbara Brown Taylor reminds us:

> *"The effort to keep faith is itself
> a form of faithfulness."*
> — *Barbara Brown Taylor, Learning to Walk in the Dark*

So maybe today, faithfulness looks
like pausing at the window.
Or choosing a gentle word when
you could have spoken sharply.
Or simply breathing, and letting
yourself be loved.

Remember, even when the way
forward is hidden, you are not lost.
You are held.

❦ A Gentle Practice

Take five minutes to sit in silence.
Breathe deeply.
Let the phrase "I am beloved" echo
in your mind.

Notice what stirs, and let it be
enough for today.

❦ A Snapshot of Grace in Real Life

Later that week, he made a small mistake—
nothing catastrophic, just
a careless comment that landed
wrong with a friend.

For a moment, the old familiar wave
of shame started to rise. In the past,
this would have sent him into a
tailspin of self-criticism and regret,

replaying the moment over and over,
searching for ways to punish himself
or make it right by sheer effort.

But this time, something was different.

He paused.
He remembered the quiet of the morning,
the gentle invitation to
grace, the truth that he was beloved—
even here, even now.

Instead of spiraling, he took a slow
breath and whispered a simple prayer:

"Jesus, I need your grace for this, too."

He felt the weight begin to lift—
not because he'd fixed the mistake,
but because he was learning to let
grace meet him in the middle of it.

He apologized to his friend,
honestly but without self-condemnation.
And then, for the first time in a long time,
he let himself move on—
grateful, lighter, quietly changed.

Maybe this is how grace works:

Not erasing our missteps, but
rescuing us from the cycle of shame
and letting us begin again.

As you finish this chapter, consider:

Where have you seen grace meet
you in a small, unexpected way?

Is there a moment this week when
you could pause, breathe, and let
God's love interrupt the old cycle?

Even the smallest step toward
grace is worth celebrating.

May you notice—and cherish—
your own quiet moments of
transformation, trusting that God's
gentle work is unfolding in you,
one day at a time.

❧ Closing Prayer for the Quiet Journey

Jesus,

Thank You for meeting me in the
slow places—
in the fog, in the quiet, in the
moments no one else sees.

Help me trust Your gentle work in me,
even when I can't measure it.

Shape my words, my choices, my heart
to reflect Your love—one quiet day
at a time.

Teach me to abide,
to rest,
to believe that Your presence is
enough.

Amen.

CHAPTER EIGHT

The Real Battle

Becoming Dangerous in the Light

❧ A Scene from the Front Lines

He didn't even see it coming.
Not this time.

It wasn't the obvious temptations.
Not lust or rage or some old pattern
he thought he'd already buried. It
was the slow, quiet ache of feeling unseen.
Forgotten. Unloved.

The thought came like a whisper:

"Does God even notice me anymore?"

That's where the real battle began.
Not in sin, but in the moment just before it—
when desire bends
toward despair, and despair reaches
for something to numb the ache.
That moment is the doorway.
That moment is war.

He sat in his car, engine off,
staring through the windshield.
Rain traced lines down the glass like tear streaks.
He hadn't done anything yet.
But he knew he could.
A choice stood before him like two roads
splitting from his soul.

And then, quietly:

"You're not alone here."

He didn't hear it with his ears,
but something deeper did.
He breathed, barely. And stayed.

This, too, was spiritual warfare.

❧ Where the Real War Begins

Spiritual warfare doesn't always feel
like battle.
Sometimes it feels like boredom.
Sometimes like longing.
Sometimes like the dull ache of not being okay.

It happens in kitchens, bedrooms,
work trucks, phone screens.
It happens when the pain of the
past meets the pressure of the present.
It happens when you're tempted not
to believe you're still worth fighting for.

James tells us:

> *"Each person is tempted when they*
> *are dragged away by their*
> *own desire and enticed. Then,*
> *after desire has conceived, it*
> *gives birth to sin; and sin, when*
> *it is full-grown, gives birth to death."*
> *— James 1:14–15*

The enemy doesn't create all temptation.
Sometimes we open the door ourselves.
But he waits just outside,
ready to amplify what we've already begun.

That's why honesty is the first weapon.

✎ The War Over Your Name

The enemy's real target is not your
behavior—it's your identity.

He opens every attack the same
way he did with Jesus:

> *"If You are the Son of God…"*
> *— Matthew 4:3*

Not "if You're powerful."
Not "if You're holy."
But: If You really belong.

Because if he can get you to
question that, he can get you to
reach for anything to prove you're worthy.

But God has already spoken a
better word:

"You are My beloved."
"You are clean."
"You are Mine."

The war is not for perfection.
The war is for your name.

⚘ The Armor

Not Magic, But Movement

Paul didn't give us a spell.
He gave us a stance.

> *"Put on the full armor of God, so*
> *that you can take your stand…"*
> *— Ephesians 6:11*

This is not about performance.
It's about remembering what's
already true and living like it's real.

Belt of Truth

→ I am not proving myself. I am
covered by Christ.

Breastplate of Righteousness

→ I move through life grounded—
not rushed, not ruled by chaos.

Shoes of the Gospel of Peace

→ I lift up trust when lies fly at me. I hold fast to what God says.

Shield of Faith

→ I guard my mind with the truth: I belong to Jesus.

Helmet of Salvation

→ I speak Scripture not as defense,
 but as truth that cuts through darkness.

Sword of the Spirit (Word of God)

→ This armor isn't for a quick recitation.
It's for a new way of living—fully clothed in Christ.

❧ The Champion Who Fights Beside You

You are not the hero of this story.
But you are in it.
And the danger is real.

You find yourself in an arena—
ancient, cracked stone rising in tiers
all around you like the mouths of a
thousand silent judges. Dust lifts in
ghostly swirls with every tremble of
your feet. The air is thick—choked

with iron, ash, and the scent of
something ancient and wrong.

You're standing in the center. Alone. Bare-handed.

Across from you, the enemy circles—
hulking, grinning, eyes glowing
with accusation. His breath reeks of
rot and sulfur. His voice is soft and serpentine,
but every word slithers deep:

"You're weak. You always give in.
This time will be no different."

Your chest tightens. You can't breathe.

You scan the stands—no faces, just shadows.
They don't speak. They don't help.
They only watch.

Your knees nearly give way.

And then… you remember:

There's another gate.

It's behind you. Heavy. Closed. But
not locked.

On the other side, He waits.
Not because He's reluctant.
But because He loves freely—and
will not force Himself in.

"God is faithful. He will not allow
you to be tempted beyond what
you can bear. And with the
temptation, He will also make a
way of escape..."
    — 1 Corinthians 10:13

You whisper it—not with strength,
but with surrender:

"Jesus... I can't win this. I need You."

That's all it takes.

Suddenly—
The glory of the King breaks
through the gate like a sunrise
tearing through a nightmare.
Light explodes into the arena,
driving back every shadow.

And there He stands.
Not silent. Not tame.
Clothed in radiance, crowned with justice,
His robe dipped in blood. His eyes are like flames of fire.
On His thigh is written King of kings and Lord of lords.
His voice is the roar of rushing waters—
drowning out every lie, every whisper, every accusation.

"Who is this King of glory?"
"The Lord, strong and mighty.
The Lord, mighty in battle."
    — Psalm 24:8

The enemy recoils, eyes wide with terror.
The ground shakes beneath your
feet. The crowd vanishes in awe.

And then the King draws His sword.
Not forged by men, but by Spirit and flame.
It is the Word of God—
a double-edged sword, alive and active,
flashing like lightning, cutting through
bone and soul, lies and legacy,
past and present.

> *"From His mouth comes a sharp sword*
> *with which to strike down the nations…"*
> — *Revelation 19:15*

> *"The Word of God is living and active,*
> *sharper than any two-edged sword…"*
> — *Hebrews 4:12*

The enemy stumbles back—not wounded, but undone.
He turns and flees from the One
who already disarmed him at the Cross.

> *"He made a public spectacle of them,*
> *triumphing over them by the Cross."*
> — *Colossians 2:15*

You fall to your knees—not in fear, but awe.
You are not just spared.
You are claimed.
You are covered.
You are loved.

And as the King stands beside you,
sword still burning with holy fire,
you realize: the war was never yours to win.
It was always His.

❧ The Weapons of the Beloved

You don't need a new strategy.
You need to pick up what was
always yours.

Real Weapons:

- Honesty – Tell the truth. Even when it costs you. Especially when it costs you.

- Surrender – You weren't made to fight alone. Invite Him in.

- Remembrance – Say who He is. Say what He's done. Say it out loud.

- Scripture – Don't just quote it. Believe it.

- Community – Don't war in silence. Bring others into your fight.

- Worship – Praise silences the accuser and welcomes the King.

*"They overcame him by the
blood of the Lamb and by the
word of their testimony."*
        — Revelation 12:11

❧ What Victory Looks Like

Victory is not perfection.
Victory is staying.

Victory is not pretending you're fine.
It's choosing honesty over hiding.
It's calling on Jesus when you still
feel weak.
It's whispering again:

"I choose love. I choose freedom. I choose You."

❧ Reflection & Application Questions

- Where have you tried to fight alone?
- What false names have you believed about yourself?
- Which piece of the armor do you need to start walking in—not just reciting?

❧ Practice

Prayer of the Beloved Warrior

Jesus,

I surrender the fight I keep
trying to win alone.
You are my victory.
You are my defender.

I choose honesty.
I choose love.
I choose to stand.

Cover me in Your truth.
Fight beside me.
Make me dangerous to darkness.

Amen.

❧ Mantra for the Battle

"I am seen. I am loved. I am held.
The battle is the Lord's."

❧ Final Blessing

The enemy does not get the last
word in your life.
Not on your worst day. Not even in your weakest moment.

You are not defined by what you've done.
You are not disqualified by what was done to you.
You are Christ's. And He never loses.

The war is real.
But so is the victory.
Walk in it.

I am seen. I am loved. I am held. The battle is the Lord's.

CHAPTER NINE

The Tower Stands

How Stillness Becomes Strength

❧ The Building That Learned to Stand

There's a building in San Francisco that leans.

The Millennium Tower—luxurious,
58 stories tall—was built with impeccable style and the best intentions.
But beneath its sleek surface was a fatal flaw: its foundation didn't reach
bedrock. Over time, it began to tilt. Engineers tried to fix it—
adding concrete, adjusting weight—but it kept sinking until they
finally did what should have been done in the beginning:
dig deep, anchor to what holds.

It didn't collapse. But it had to be corrected.

So did he.

❧ The Stillness That Speaks

He didn't notice the silence at first.

At the workbench, surrounded by
scrap wood and old screws, the

man had become used to a certain
ache. It used to scream. Now it whispered. The shop light buzzed
above him, soft and golden, as
sawdust hovered in the quiet like suspended memory.

He wiped his hands on a rag and
exhaled. No rush. No shame nipping
at his heels. Just stillness.

He thought of his failures—not with panic or self-loathing, but with
gentle clarity. Like looking at a
photo of someone he used to know. There had been shouting matches,
slammed doors, nights lost to darkness. Once, he remembered, his wife
had flinched when he raised his voice.

Now she reached for his hand.

❧ The Difference Others See

Later that week, the man stood in
the kitchen drying a plate when she walked in. She paused—not in fear,
but in awareness. There was
something different about him now.
He didn't try so hard to impress her.
He just stood there—present, unhurried.

She smiled. He smiled back.
That was all.

They didn't need to name it. But
they both knew: the house no
longer leaned.

That evening, his phone buzzed. A friend. One of those friends who
never really asked for help before.

He answered. "Hey."

There was a long pause on the
other end, then a broken voice said,
"I messed up bad."

He listened.
Not with answers. Not with advice.
With presence.

When the silence came again,
he simply said, "I've been there."

He had no idea that those three
words would become someone
else's new foundation.

❧ What's Different Now?

It wasn't about doing more.
It was about being different. Rooted. Real.

He had moved from trying harder to trusting deeper.
From shame-based striving to grace-based standing.
From performing for love to living
from love.
From avoiding failure to learning from failure.
From running alone to walking
together.

He wasn't perfect. But he was
anchored.

Like the tower, he didn't need to be flawless—just founded on
something deeper.

❧ Lectio Divina

Slow Down and Listen

> *"I waited patiently for the Lord;*
> *He turned to me and heard my cry.*
> *He lifted me out of the slimy pit,*
> *out of the mud and mire;*
> *He set my feet on a rock and*
> *gave me a firm place to stand."*
> *— Psalm 40:1–2*

Read it again—slowly. Pause after
each line.

Now pray:

"Lord, thank You for turning toward me. Thank You for lifting me.
I no longer live in the pit.
I stand—because You have made me stand."

Breathe deep.
He has made your steps firm.

❧ Reflection Questions

- Where do you still feel "tilted" in life?
- Have you asked God to dig deeper?
- What voices used to define you that no longer have power?
- Who has seen the difference in you—and how might you invite them into their own rebuilding?

❧ Practice of Formation

Let Others See

Joy multiplies when shared.

Take one simple risk this week:

- Share your "leaning tower" story with someone
- Ask God who needs to see the evidence of your restoration
- Let someone know: "He dug deep, and now I stand"

This kind of rebuilding isn't done alone.
The healing you share may become
someone else's new foundation.

❧ Words from the Way

> *"The aim of God in history is the creation of an all-inclusive community of loving persons with God Himself at the very center of this community as its prime Sustainer and most glorious Inhabitant."*
> — *Dallas Willard*

"Joy does not simply happen to us. We have to choose joy and keep choosing it every day."
— *Henri Nouwen*

❧ Prayer of Praise and Thanksgiving

Jesus, You are my foundation.
You have made me stand.

I remember the pit—
and I thank You for pulling me out.

I remember the shame—
and I thank You for calling me by
name.

I remember the silence—
and I thank You for filling it with Your peace.

My tower still stands—not because
of me,
but because You dug deep and
reached bedrock.

I am anchored now.
I will not be moved.

Thank You, Lord.

Amen.

CHAPTER TEN

The Light Left On

❧ The Workshop of Redemption

The garage was different now.

Clean, but not perfect—sawdust still
traced the seams of the concrete,
and fresh dust danced in the beams
of sunlight pouring through the window.

The filtered light caught it midair,
making it shimmer like
incense rising with the music.
Worship songs played from the old
speaker in the corner—today it was
"Goodness of God," the lyrics low
but insistent, echoing like a promise.

He had swept the shop, but not too much.
The sacredness wasn't in eliminating the past,
but in working in the midst of it.
The same space that had once held him in collapse
now held him upright.
His workbench was alive again.

An old table lay on its side in the
middle of the room.
The legs were scuffed, one cracked near the base.
His wife had asked him to fix it months ago.
Back then, he couldn't even lift it.
Now, his hands moved with calm.

Sandpaper in one hand,
the other resting on the wood,
he worked slowly, as if redeeming more
than just furniture.

As he worked, he was talking to the Lord—
out loud, gently, the way one talks to someone they trust. He
wasn't asking for rescue anymore.
He was thanking Him. A verse rose
in his mind as he pressed into the grain:

"The joy of the Lord is my strength."

It wasn't adrenaline joy. It was
rooted. Durable. The kind that
rebuilds a man from the inside out.

There was a scrap of wood sitting
near the window—he picked it up,
ran his fingers over the writing he had
scrawled on it with a marker
during a men's retreat, long before
any of this had made sense. The
letters were still legible, the grain of
the wood still rough.

"Man goes deeper to be higher;
discovers heaven on his knees."

He smiled. Back then, it had felt like
a headline of hope he couldn't
reach. Now, it felt like a journal entry—
truth written in his own story.

The table leg creaked a little as he
reset it. He pressed the new wood
into the split, gluing and clamping it tight. Then he whispered:

"Not forgotten. Just broken. And
being remade."

❧ The Family Table

Behind him, the door creaked open.

His wife peeked in, a faint smirk on
her face.

"I didn't come just to check on the table," she said softly.

Her voice was playful, but
something tender sat beneath it.

She walked over, brushing her hand along the table's edge.

"I've missed this," she said, not just meaning the shop. "I've missed you."

He didn't speak at first. He just nodded and put his hand over hers.
Their fingers rested on the table's surface like a silent vow. She leaned in
close, resting her head on his shoulder for a breath.

Their son stepped in behind her,
holding two bottles of root beer.

"Mom said you were fixing something. Can I help?"

He looked up at his boy and smiled. "Sure. Want to hand me those
clamps?"

The boy set down the bottles and scrambled over.
For a moment, they all hovered over
the same worn table—mother, father, son. Tools
passed hand to hand. Smiles
passed back and forth. The music
played low in the background, and
there was laughter in the sawdust.

Not the roaring kind. The warm kind. Like joy had found its home.

As they worked, the boy whispered something silly. His father
chuckled, tossed back a line of his own. The
boy cackled, beaming, wiping dust
on his pants. Even his mom joined
in, shaking her head and saying,
"You two are hopeless." But she
said it with tears in her eyes—tears
of healing, of wonder.

Later, the boy stood beside the
man, leaning on the bench,
mimicking his posture.
The father looked down at his son and saw
himself again. But this time, not alone.

The three of them worked together—
not just on the table, but on
something invisible. Something permanent. Restoration.

⚘ The Light Left On

Then, the door creaked again.
No knock.
Just presence.

The man looked toward it. No one
was there. But he knew.

Christ had always been in this room.
But now He was close enough to feel.

And still, the man stood a moment
longer after everyone had gone.
He ran his hand once more over the
inscription on the old scrap of wood.
This was where it had started.
On the floor, in the dark,
in despair. And now—

Now it was light.

He walked to the switch by the door.
His hand hovered. Then stopped.

He left the light on.

Outside, his wife was waiting. His
son had run ahead. He stepped into

the sunlight and gently closed the
garage door behind him.

❧ Final Reflection

You, too, may find yourself returning
to the place where it all unraveled.
And when you do, it might look
different—not because the place
has changed, but because you have.

Maybe the light in your soul is back on.
Maybe the music plays again.
Maybe, just maybe, you are being rebuilt.

Some days the tower still creaks.
But now you know where to turn
when it does.

You don't have to be perfect to walk forward.
You only have to be honest, and ready.

And if you ever forget where the
journey began—remember this:

He never left.
He just waited for the light to be
turned on.

The Book on the Table

❧ A Meeting Over Coffee

He sat at the back of a nearly empty
café, watching raindrops slide down
the window like droplets of grace.
A half-finished cappuccino cooled
before him; worship music drifted
from hidden speakers.

Across the table, a younger man—
eyes rimmed with tears, jaw tight—
clutched a paper cup he hadn't
touched. Everything about him was braced.

They'd barely met. A mutual friend
had connected them. The older man
simply nodded, then reached into
his satchel and drew out a copy of
this very book.

❧ The Offering

He laid it on the table as gently as a dove's wing.

"I wrote this," he said softly, "not because I had all the answers, but
because I was once where you are
now. I needed my way back—not to religion, but to Love."

The younger man ran his fingers
over the cover, pausing at the
scrap-wood image burned into the margin—
the familiar retreat slogan:

"Man goes deeper to be higher;
discovers heaven on his knees."

He looked up. "What happened to you?"

The older man's smile was quiet,
full of peace. "I met Him again in the
place I thought He'd abandoned me.
I found He was never gone—just waiting."

❧ The Invitation

Silence stretched between them
before the older man spoke again:

"Read it. Take your time.
And when you're ready, come by the shop. I'll
be fixing more tables—that's how healing spreads."

He rose, tapped the book, and added:

"He's coming after you. You don't
have to chase Him—just let Him in."

Then he stepped into the rain, hood
up, pace unhurried.

❧ The Light Began to Turn On

Behind him, the younger man
opened the book. The pages fell
open to a passage that felt like home—
words of grace, chapters of healing,
an invitation to stay in the
light.

And in that moment, the light began
to turn on.

About the Author

G. Wray writes from the road—literally. Alongside his wife, a fellow writer and his most trusted sounding board, he travels across the United States, Canada, and Alaska as a long-haul trucker. But his true vocation is not merely crossing miles—it's helping people find their way back to the God who never left.

After years of living with silent wounds and a faith that felt distant, he began the long road home—through doubt, through pain, and into the gentle truth of Christ's love. This book was born not from theological theory, but from lived experience, hard-won healing, and sacred conversation.

When he's not behind the wheel or behind the words, he's usually somewhere listening, learning, or encouraging someone to take the next honest step.